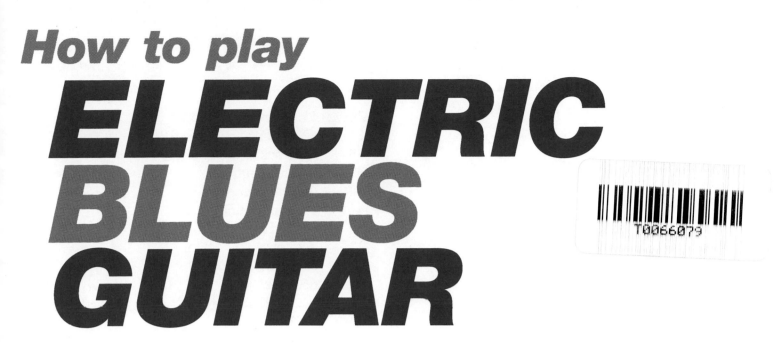

How to play
ELECTRIC BLUES GUITAR

by Alan Warner.
*Learn how to play blues guitar
like a pro from a pro!*

Interior design and layout: Len Vogler

Order No. AM 962490
US International Standard Book Number: 0.8256.1793.6
UK International Standard Book Number: 0.7119.8023.3

Exclusive Distributors:
Music Sales Corporation
257 Park Avenue South, New York, NY 10010 USA
Music Sales Limited
8/9 Frith Street, London W1V 5TZ England
Music Sales Pty. Limited
120 Rothschild Street, Rosebery, Sydney, NSW 2018, Australia

Printed in the United States of America by
Vicks Lithograph and Printing Corporation

Amsco Publications
New York/London/Paris/Sydney/Copenhagen/Madrid

COMPACT DISC TRACK LISTING

Contents

Basic Theory

Here is some basic theory to help you become more knowledgeable about the guitar fingerboard. The more theory you know, the easier it is to expand on your own musical ideas.
Look at the G major scale below; the first note is G (root note) and is called the *first degree* of the scale. The second note is A, known as the *second degree* of the scale. The degrees of the scale continue on through B, C, D, E, and F♯, until you reach G again. This G is the same as the root note one octave higher. In simple terms, the notes of the G major scale look like this.

1	2	3	4	5	6	7	(1)
G	A	B	C	D	E	F♯	G

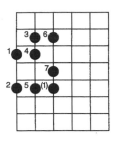

This scale pattern can be played anywhere on the fingerboard and the degree numbers will still be the same, although the key will be different. For example, if the scale was moved along so that it started at the eighth fret, the root note would be C. Therefore, the scale would be a C major scale.

But how do you know that the eighth fret position is C? If you don't know how to do this already, then now is the time to learn.
Here's a fingerboard chart showing the sixth-string fret notes. Start learning these notes by heart as soon as possible.

There are other notes in between the notes in the chart above. These notes are called *sharps* and *flats* (♯=sharp, ♭=flat) and are included in the next fingerboard chart. You'll notice that each of these notes may be known by either a sharp name or a flat name. For example, A♯ is the same note as B♭ because A♯ is one fret (half-step) higher than A and B♭ is one fret (half-step) lower than B. Because the space between B and C and the space between E and F are already half steps, there aren't any sharps or flats between either of these two sets of adjacent notes.

Finally we come to the full fingerboard chart, which as you will see is very complicated. I would just use this as a reference chart for the time being rather than trying to learn it by heart—you will come to know all of the fingerboard notes eventually.

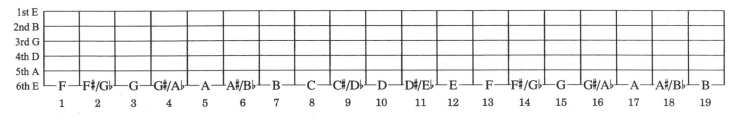

MUSIC NOTATION AND TABLATURE

If you can read music you will find standard musical notation is included in the book. The treble staff is on top and the tablature is underneath.

E = first string
B = second string
G = third string
D = fourth string
A = fifth string
E = sixth string

This is how the notes appear on the stave and tablature. (The number on each tablature line represents a fret number).

Barlines divide the music into sections containing an equal number of counts depending on the time signature at the start of the music. A barline appears at the beginning and at the end of each *measure*.

The symbol $\frac{4}{4}$ at the start of the music indicates 4 counts in each bar and is known as the time signature. You will also see the $\frac{12}{8}$ time signature at the start of some of the exercises and solos throughout the book.

TIME VALUES OF NOTES AND RESTS

Notes

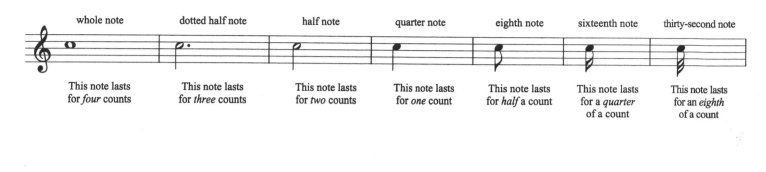

whole note	dotted half note	half note	quarter note	eighth note	sixteenth note	thirty-second note
This note lasts for *four* counts	This note lasts for *three* counts	This note lasts for *two* counts	This note lasts for *one* count	This note lasts for *half* a count	This note lasts for a *quarter* of a count	This note lasts for an *eighth* of a count

Rests

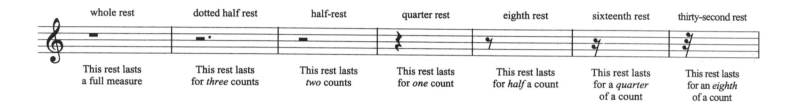

whole rest	dotted half rest	half-rest	quarter rest	eighth rest	sixteenth rest	thirty-second rest
This rest lasts a full measure	This rest lasts for *three* counts	This rest lasts *two* counts	This rest lasts for *one* count	This rest lasts for *half* a count	This rest lasts for a *quarter* of a count	This rest lasts for an *eighth* of a count

Beams

Eighth, sixteenth, and thirty-second notes are often joined by beams.

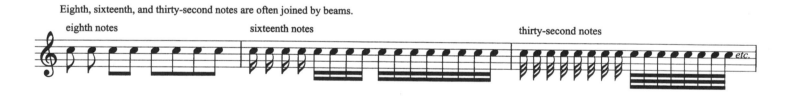

Repeat Signs

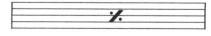

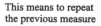

This means to repeat the previous measure

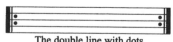

The double line with dots means to go back to the beginning of the music or repeat section enclosed by double lines and dots.

The double lines indicate the end of a section or the entire piece.

LEGEND OF MUSICAL SYMBOLS

Hammer-on
A hammer-on is where you sound a note as normal then hammer your left-hand finger down hard on the next note. ⌐ means hammer-on (⌐ = downstroke).

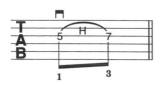

Pull-off
The pull-off is achieved by pulling your left-hand finger down off the string to create the next note. ⌐ means pull-off.

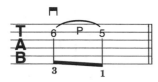

Trill
A trill effect is produced by performing hammer-ons and pull-offs in rapid succession.

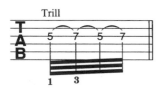

Slide going up
Sound the first note and slide up to the next (higher) note. Sl. means slide up.

Slide coming down
Sound the first note and slide down to the next (lower) note. Sl. means slide down.

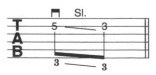

Upward string bend
First, sound the note, then push the string up to raise its pitch. The note in parentheses indicates the pitch. An upward string bend will normally be on the first, second, or third strings.
↑ arrow indicates upward string bend.

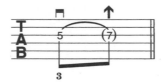

Downward string bend
For a downward string bend, pull the string down to raise pitch. A downward string bend will normally be on the third, fourth, fifth, or sixth strings.
↓ arrow indicates downward string bend.

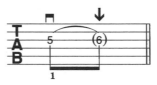

Release string bend
Return bent note back to its normal position after performing a string bend. R = release string bend.

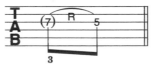

Pre-bend
The note is already bent up or down before being struck. When it has been struck you then release back down in pitch. (The note in parentheses is the pre-bent note.)

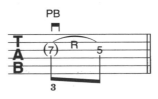

Vibrato
To create a vibrato effect, first sound the note and then rock the string from side to side.
A ～～ appears above the note.

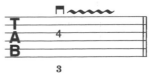

RHYTHM AND BLUES

Rhythm is an essential part of the blues guitar sound—it lays the groundwork for everything you play whether it be a riff, song, or solo. Here I'd like to start with a couple of basic chord riffs using the following chords:

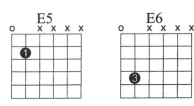

Don't sound the strings that have an **x** above them.

The first riff has a straight feel rhythm ♪♩ and the second riff has a shuffle feel rhythm ♪♪. Notice the count procedure indicated under the tablature.

1. Straight Feel Rhythm

Try resting the side of your picking hand lightly across the strings at the bridge as you strike the strings, this will give a more chunky sound.
Count 1 & 2 & 3 & 4, *etc.,* and maintain a steady beat throughout.

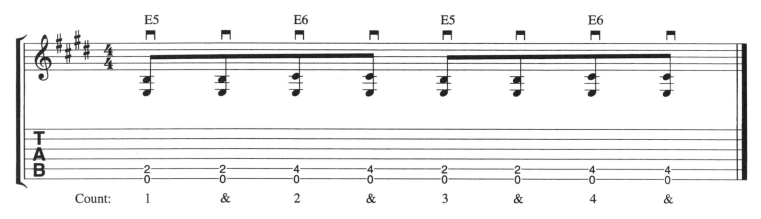

2. Shuffle Feel Rhythm

For the shuffle rhythm try counting 1 & a 2 & a, *etc.* Then try counting again, but this time leave out the & stroke so it becomes 1 (&) a 2 (&) a, *etc.*

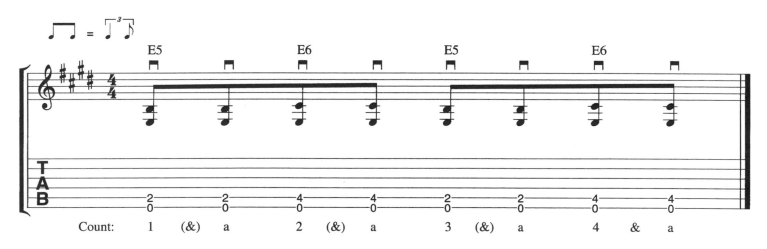

Here are some more chord riffs to learn, they all use the shuffle feel rhythm.

3. A Chord Riff

These two chords are used in this riff.

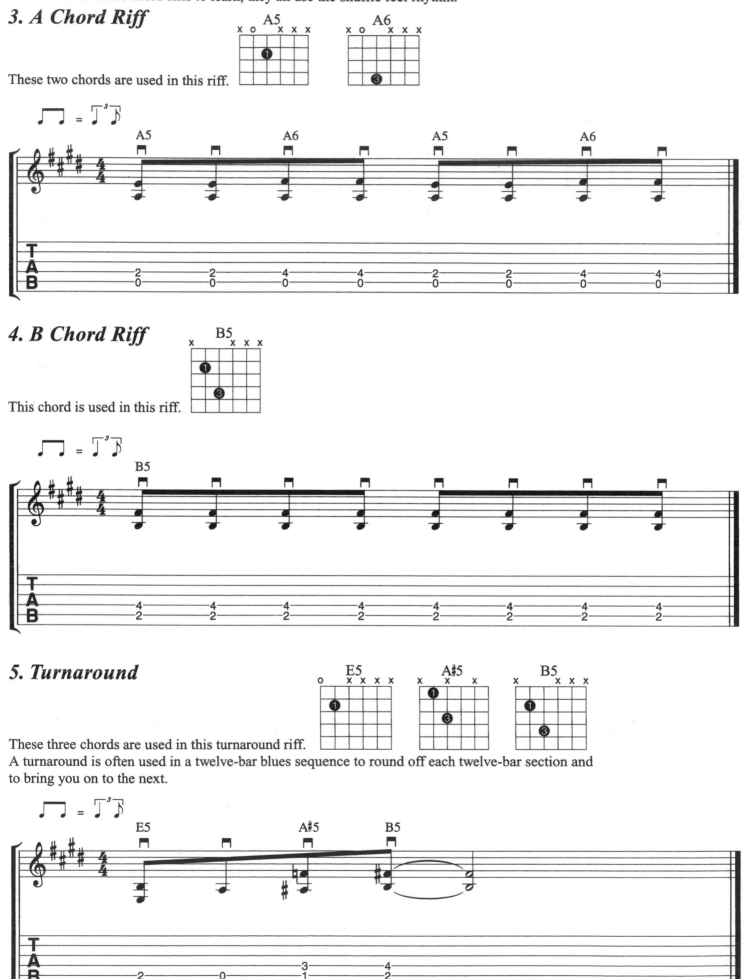

4. B Chord Riff

This chord is used in this riff.

5. Turnaround

These three chords are used in this turnaround riff.
A turnaround is often used in a twelve-bar blues sequence to round off each twelve-bar section and to bring you on to the next.

6. Twelve-Bar Shuffle

We'll put chord riffs 2, 3, 4, and 5 together now to make up the twelve-bar sequence shown here.
Remember to concentrate on your timing and rhythm throughout.

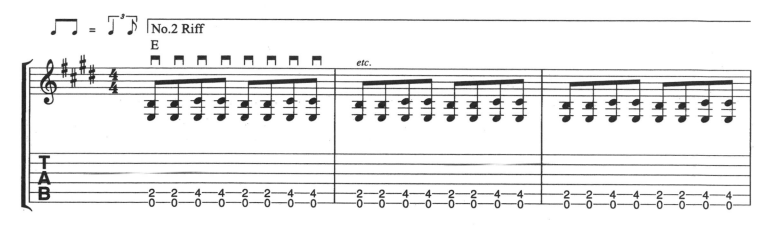

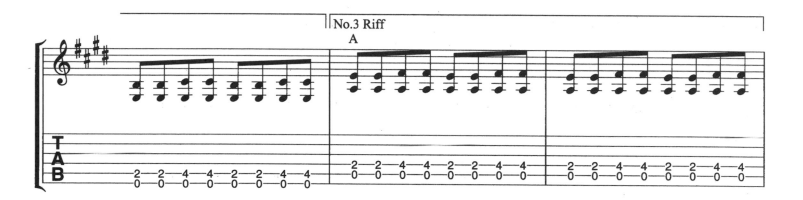

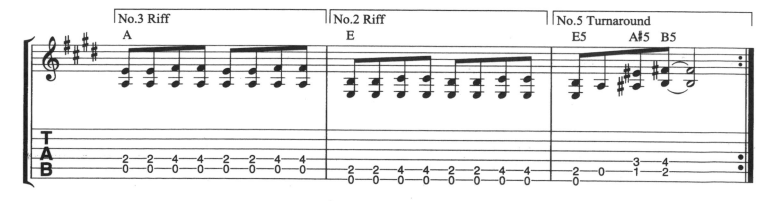

THE BLUES NOTES

A lot of blues music is based on just five notes, these notes (or tones) make up the *minor pentatonic scale* (penta = five, tonic = tone). The numbers below refer to the degrees of the major scale in any key.
The notes are as follows:

1	♭3	4	5	♭7	(1)
G	B♭	C	D	F	G

The following two fingerboard charts show where you can play the G minor pentatonic scale. Notice how the notes fit inside the box—this is known as the box pattern.

7. G Minor Pentatonic Scale

This scale is played on the lower strings, starting at the third fret of the sixth string.

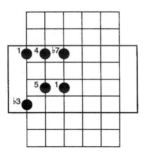

8. G Minor Pentatonic Scale

This scale is played on the higher strings starting at the fifth fret of the fourth string.

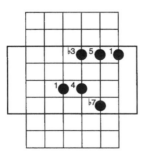

EASY BLUES PATTERNS

These two easy blues patterns are based on the notes from the G minor pentatonic scale.

9. Blues Pattern

This pattern uses the lower notes of the G minor pentatonic scale.

10. Blues Pattern

This pattern uses the higher notes of the G minor pentatonic scale.

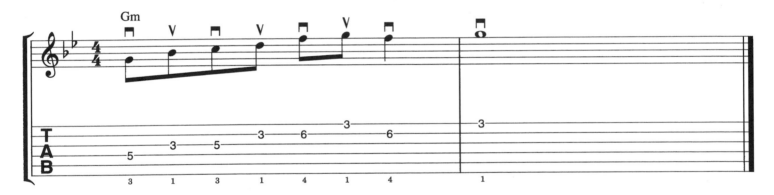

Here are three more easy blues patterns for you to learn, again, using the notes from the G minor pentatonic scale.

11. Blues Pattern

The higher notes of the G minor pentatonic scale are used to make up this pattern.

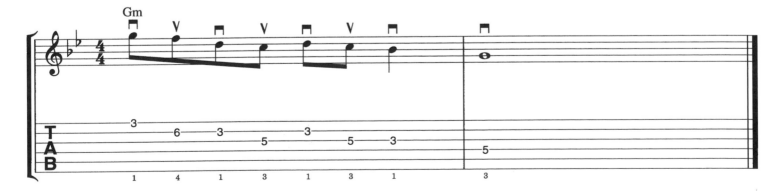

12. Blues Pattern

Just pick downwards for this very easy pattern.

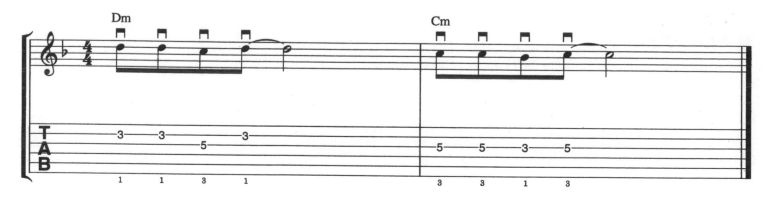

13. Turnaround

A descending run of notes combining the higher and lower strings are used for this turnaround pattern.

14. Easy Blues Solo

The patterns from pages 13 and 14 are used to form this easy guitar solo, notice that pattern number 10 is played against both the Gm and Cm chords.
Remember to concentrate on your timing and rhythm throughout.

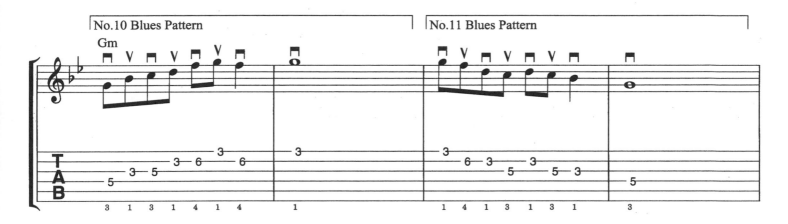

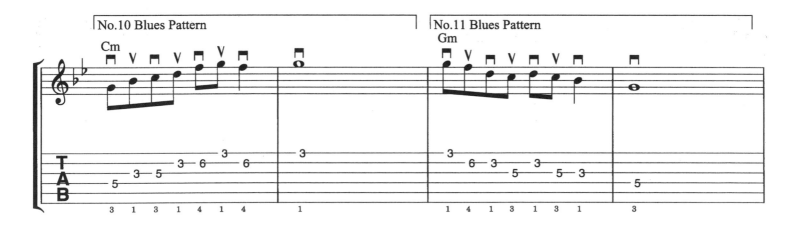

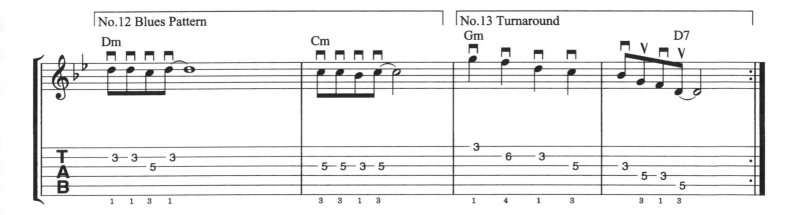

THE BLUES SCALE

To make things more bluesy and exciting we'll add another note to the minor pentatonic scale. This note appears between the third and fourth notes of the scale and can be referred to as the *b5* "flat five" or "flatted fifth." With this extra note on board we now have the famous *blues scale*.

1	b3	4	b5	5	b7
G	Bb	C	Db	D	F

15. G Blues Scale

This scale is played on the lower strings starting at the third fret of the sixth string.

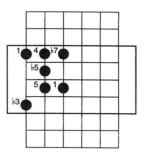

16. G Blues Scale

The following pattern shows the higher notes of the G blues scale.
The scale is played on the higher strings starting at the fifth fret of the fourth string.

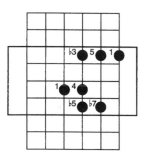

BLUES PATTERNS

The following blues patterns are derived from the blues scale and include vibrato, pull-off and hammer-on techniques (look at the "Legend of Musical Symbols" on page 8).

17. G Blues Pattern

This pattern uses the higher notes of the G blues scale and features a vibrato at the end.

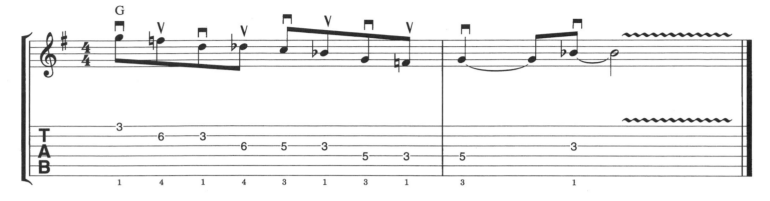

18. Blues Pattern

The lower notes of the G blues scale form this pattern which features vibratos and a pull-off.

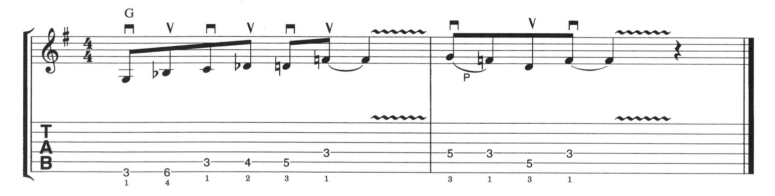

19. A Blues Pattern

We'll move up a couple of frets for this pattern so that the notes are from the A blues scale. A couple of hammer-ons and vibratos are used here.

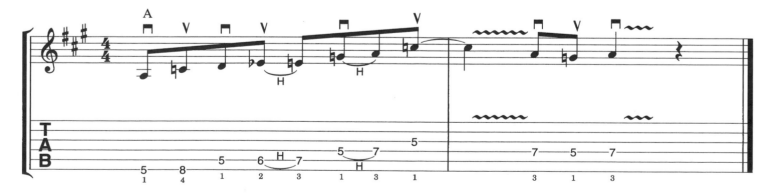

STRING BENDING

String bends are essential to the blues guitar style because they add feel and emotion to the music.

20. Upward String Bend

The example here shows a string bend on the third string. Here the string is fretted at the seventh fret with the third finger (have your second finger alongside this finger for added strength). You then strike the string and bend the string upwards to raise the pitch until it sounds two frets higher, equivalent to the ninth fret.

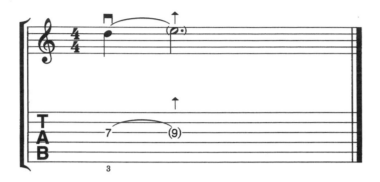

21. Downward Blues Bend

A slightly bent string is often referred to as a blues bend. Use your first finger to bend the third string downward to raise the pitch slightly.

22. Upward Bend & Release

You can also let the string come back to the original pitch after bending, this is indicated by a release symbol.

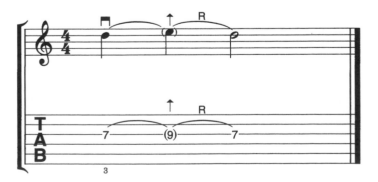

COMMON STRING BEND POSITIONS

The scale pattern below shows some of the common string bending positions used in blues and rock guitar playing.

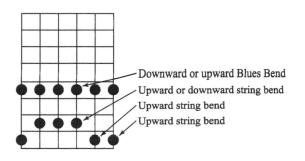

Downward or upward Blues Bend
Upward or downward string bend
Upward string bend
Upward string bend

Blues Licks with String Bends

Here are some blues licks for you to try, each lick features the string bend technique.

23. Blues Lick

An upward string bend is used in this lick. Work at obtaining a smooth positive bend.

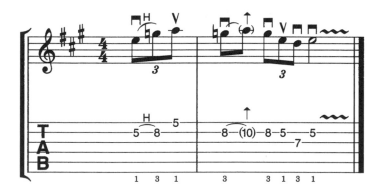

24. Blues Lick

An upward string bend is followed by a release bend and a downward blues bend here.

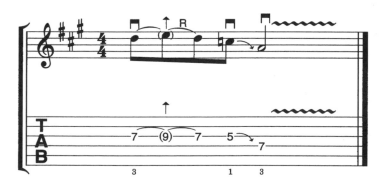

25. Blues Lick

This lick starts with an upward string bend on the third string. Notice the grace note (♪) at the start of the bend.

26. Blues Lick

You'll find this one a bit harder because the string is bent at the eighth fret of the first string which is tauter than the other strings.

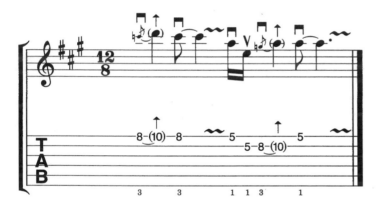

BREAKING AWAY FROM THE BOX PATTERN

So far we've been confined to playing patterns and licks inside the box. The examples that follow show how you can break away from this. One way is to use the slide technique (refer to the slide symbols on page 8).

27. G Blues Pattern

First of all study the following box blues pattern.

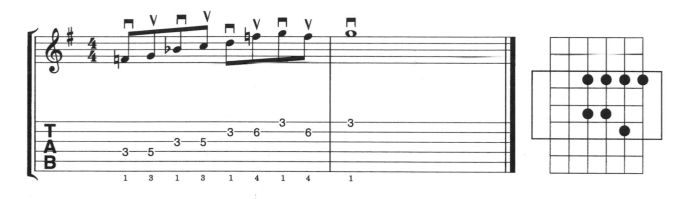

28. G Blues Pattern

Now try the same pattern again, but this time when you play the last note of the first bar (sixth fret of the second string) slide your finger along to the eighth fret instead of going to the third fret of the first string. (Notice the left-hand third finger is used for the slide instead of the fourth finger.)

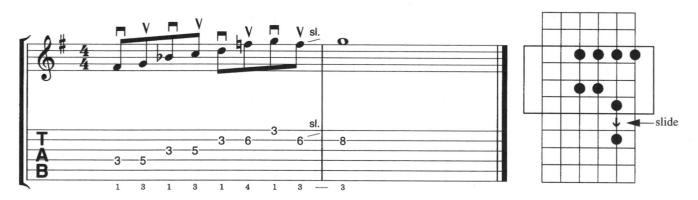

As you can see we've just covered a span of six frets which is a small step towards learning the entire fretboard.

29. G Blues Pattern

Now try going a bit further with the next pattern shown here.

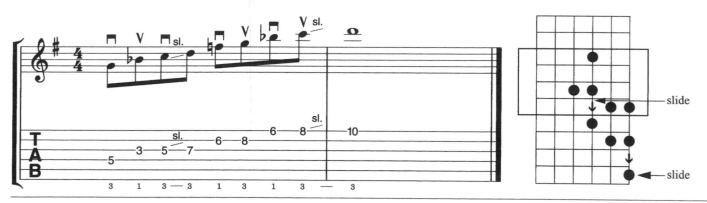

30. Ascending Blues Run

Now try this ascending run which starts at the fifth fret of the sixth string and finishes at the tenth fret of the second string. The notes are based on the A minor pentatonic scale:

1	♭3	4	5	♭7
A	C	D	E	G

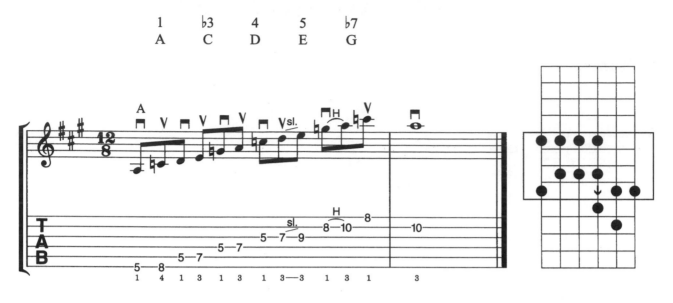

31. Descending Blues Run

This descending blues run starts at the tenth fret of the second string and finishes at the fifth fret of the sixth string. The notes are from the A blues scale:

1,	♭3,	4,	♭5,	5,	♭7
A	C	D	E♭	E	G

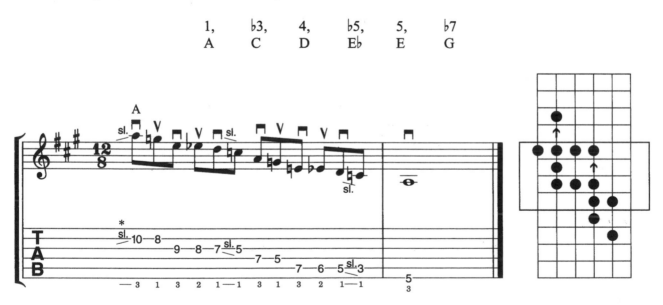

A very fast slide that doesn't start from a specific note.

PREPARATION FOR *URBAN BLUES SOLO*

The following blues licks and runs are used in the next guitar solo on pages 24 and 25.

32. Urban Blues Lick

Here's a very easy lick for you although it needs to be played with tight precision.

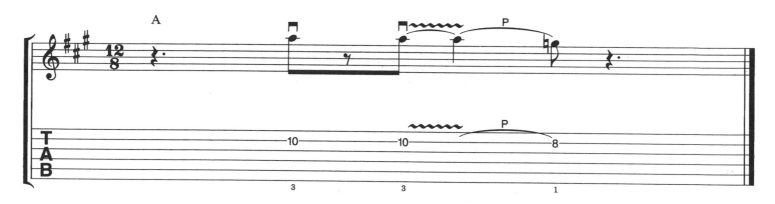

33. Descending Blues Run

This run is the same as number 31 on page 22 except for the last note.

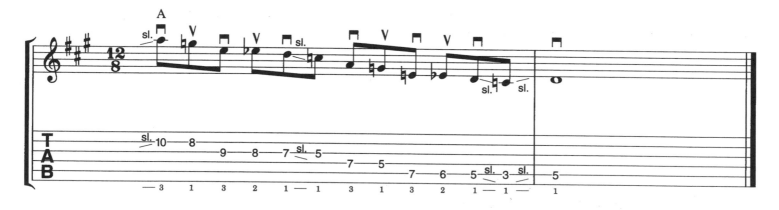

34. Urban Blues Lick

There's quite a few things going on here in this lick, you may find it best to master the first half of the lick before tackling the rest.

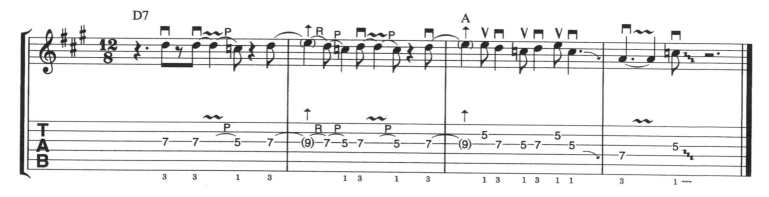

35. Blues Lick Featuring Doublestops

You will have to swap your first finger (last note of bar one) with your third finger (same note at the start of bar two) to enable you to play the rest of this lick properly, notice the bluesy sounding double-stops (two-note chord) at the end.

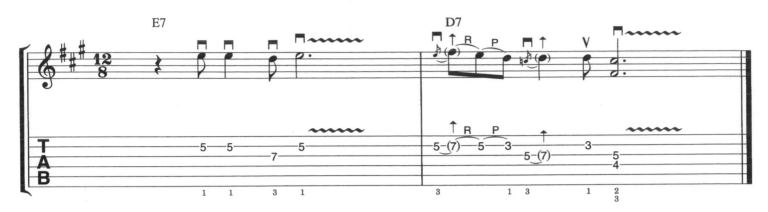

36. Ascending Blues Run and Turnaround

This is the same as ascending blues run number 30 on page 22 but with a turnaround at the end, notice the upward blues bend on the second note of the turnaround.

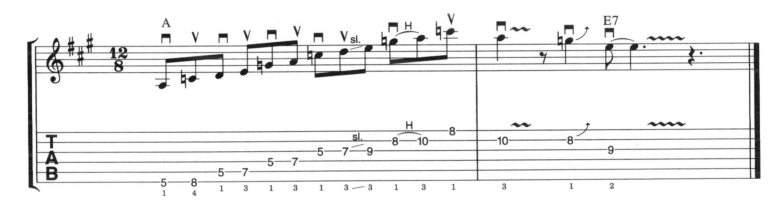

37. Urban Blues Solo

If you have mastered the blues licks and runs from pages 23 and 24 you shouldn't have too much difficulty learning this solo.
The solo is played twice with a turnaround at the end of the first twelve bars and an outro at the end. Have fun.

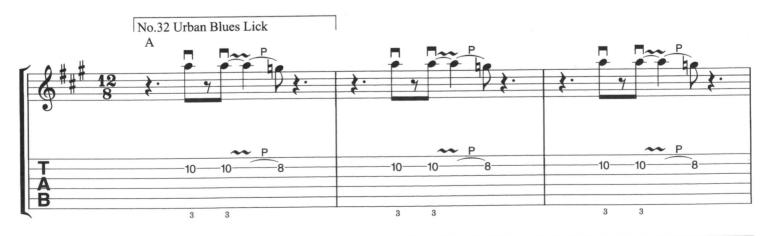

No.33 Descending Blues Run

No.34 Urban Blues Lick

No.34 continued

No.35 Blues Lick Featuring Double Stops

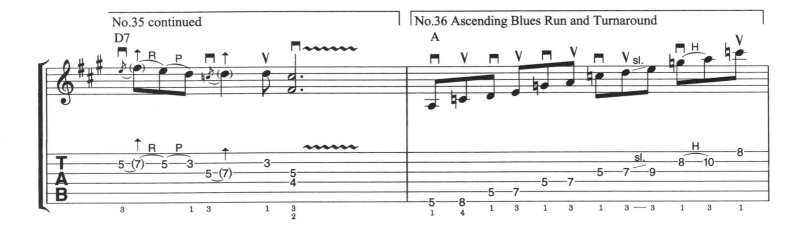

No.35 continued

No.36 Ascending Blues Run and Turnaround

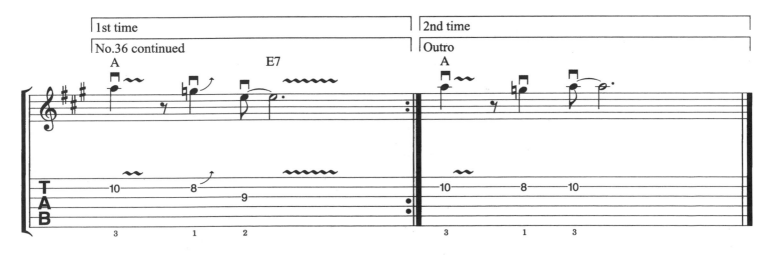

1st time

No.36 continued

2nd time

Outro

BLUES PROGRESSIONS

There is a common belief that all blues songs and solos are made up of twelve bars containing three chords, this is definitely not so as you will see from the two examples shown below. These are both classic eight-bar blues progressions with lots of interesting chord changes throughout.

38. Eight-Bar Blues Progression

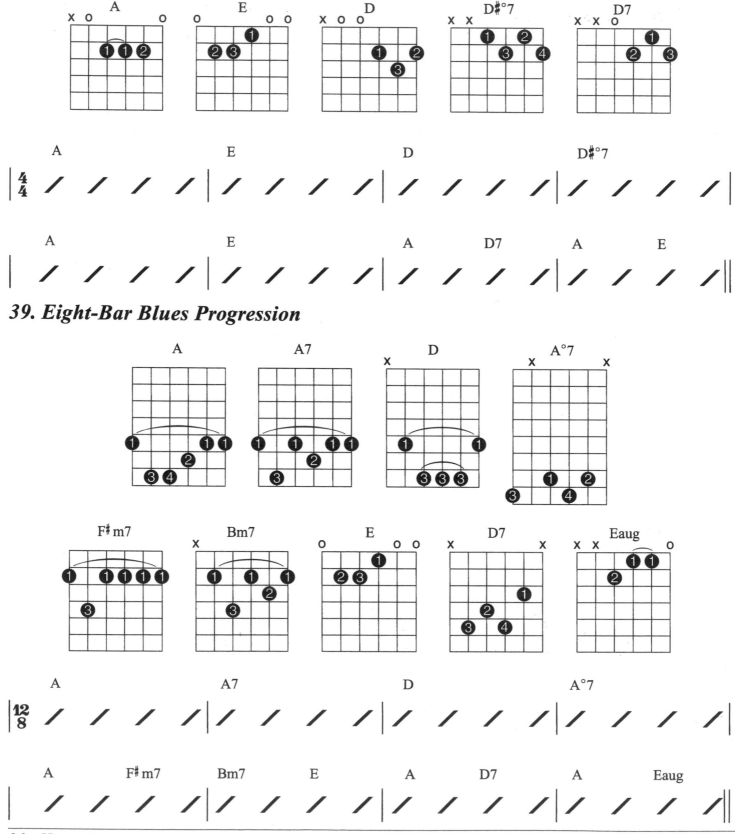

39. Eight-Bar Blues Progression

PREPARATION FOR OPEN ROAD BLUES

The next solo—*Open Road Blues* on pages 28 and 29—is played over eight-bar blues progression number 38 and uses the licks shown here.

40. Blues Lick

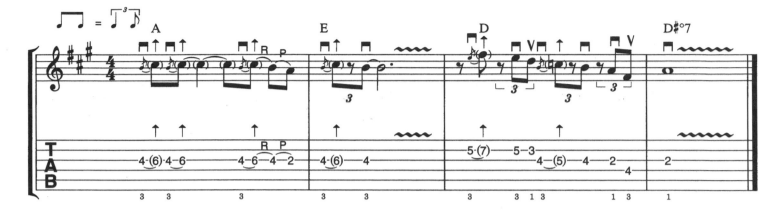

41. Blues Lick and Turnaround

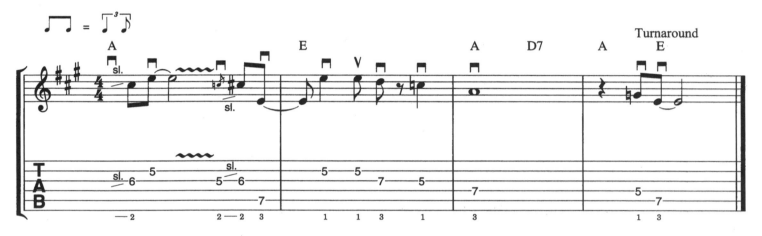

42. Outro Lick

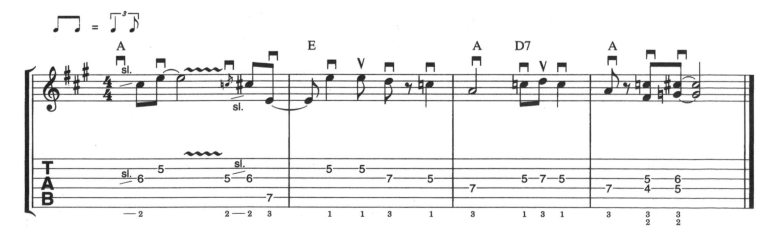

43. Open Road Blues

Open Road Blues is a lively paced solo consisting of two verses. Both verses are the same except that one has a turnaround at the end and the other has an outro to finish the solo.

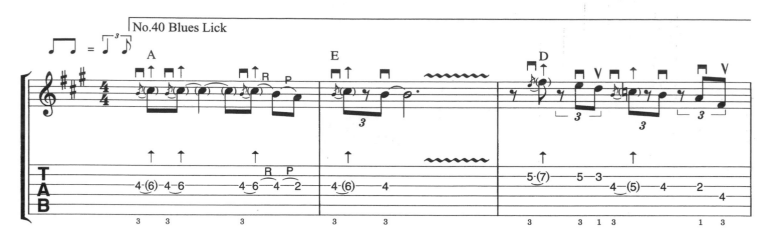

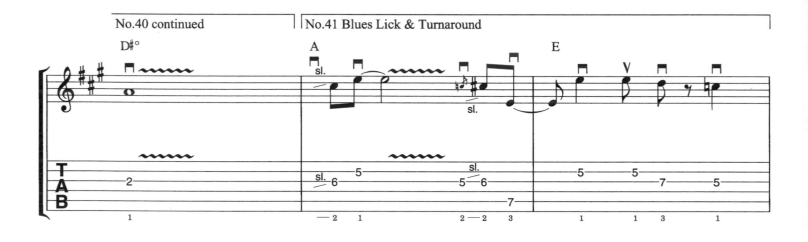

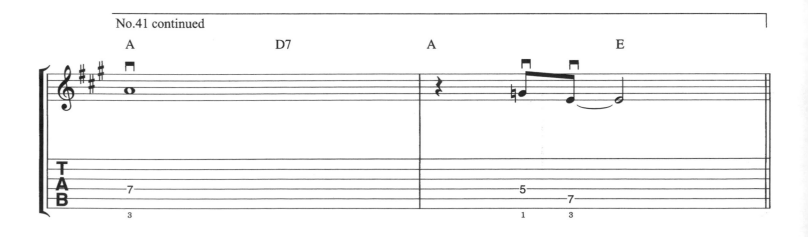

No.40 Blues Lick

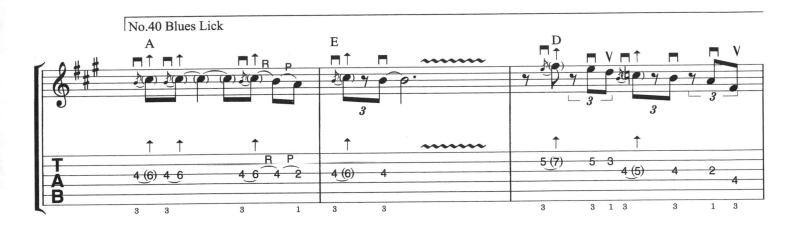

No.40 continued

No.42 Outro Lick

No.42 continued

Preparation for *A.W. Blues*

These blues licks are used in the next guitar solo *A.W. Blues* which is based on eight-Bar Blues progression number 39 from page 26.

44. Blues Lick

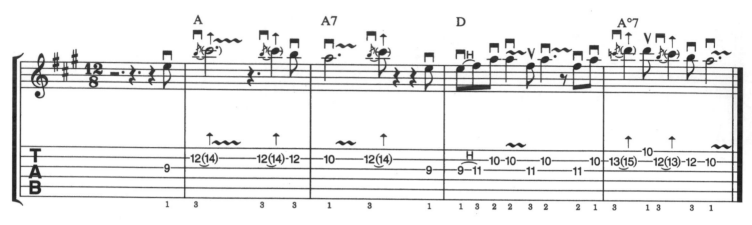

45. Blues Lick and Turnaround

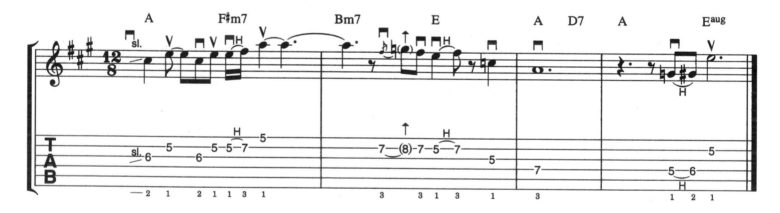

46. Outro Lick

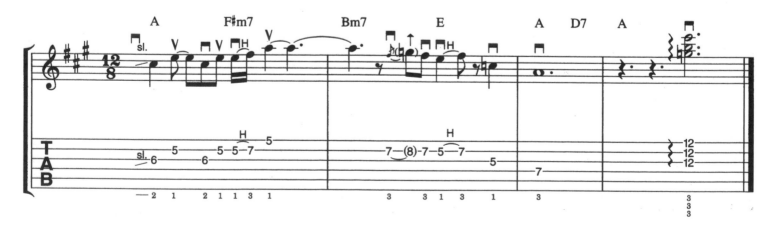

47. A.W. Blues

This solo is quite straightforward. There are two verses, the first verse is made up of licks 44 and 45 and the second verse uses licks 44 and 46 although the first note of lick number 44 is left out this time.

Verse One

No.44 Blues Lick

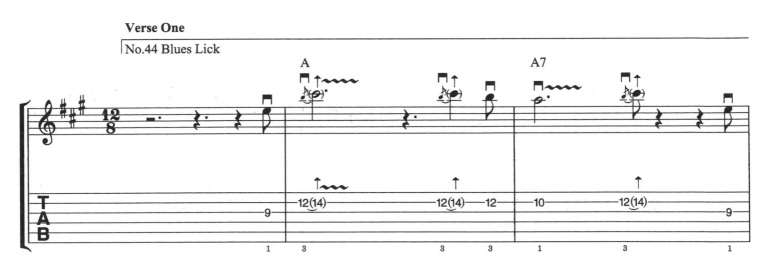

No.44 continued

No.45 Blues Lick & Turnaround

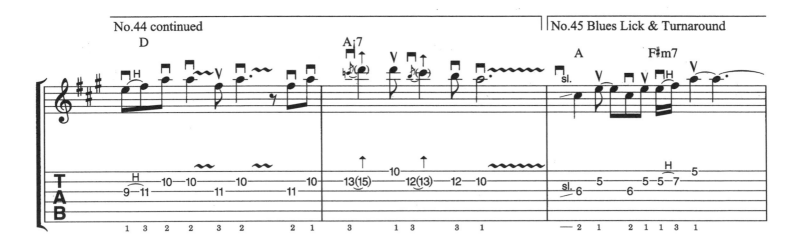

No.45 continued

Turnaround

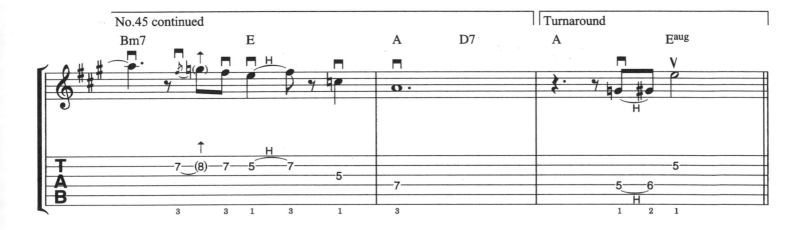

No.44 Blues Lick (First note omitted)

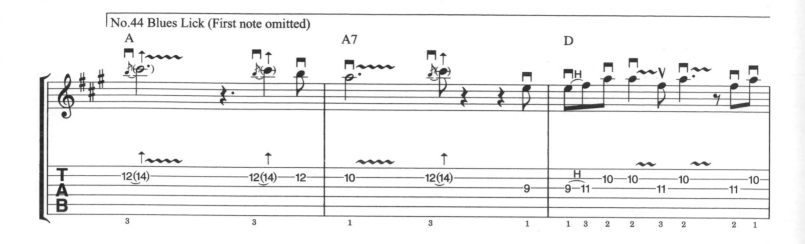

No.44 continued

No.46 Outro Lick

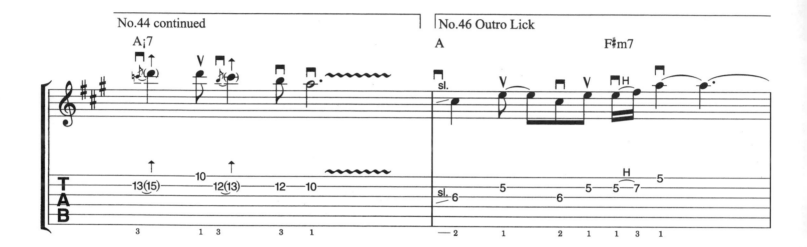

No.46 continued

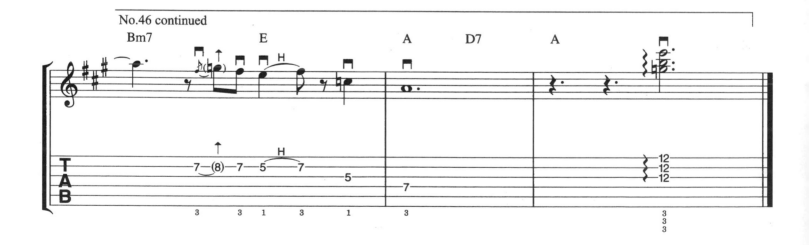

MORE SCALES

The two scales shown here have a happier sound compared to the minor pentatonic and blues scales shown earlier in the book. Both are laid out in two-octave fashion so all of the strings are used.

48. G Major Pentatonic Scale

The notes of this five note scale are:

1	2	3	5	6
G	A	B	D	E

Listen to the opening riff to Smokey Robinson's, *My Girl* which is based on this scale.

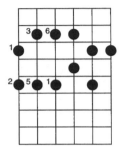

49. G Mixolydian Scale

This is a seven-note scale and the notes are:

1	2	3	4	5	6	♭7
G	A	B	C	D	E	F

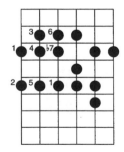

CHORD RIFFS

Here are some riffs based on chords which I think you'll enjoy learning. The first one uses these two chords.

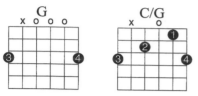

Its important that you try to stop the fifth string from sounding. Do this by touching it with your third finger. It may take a bit of practice if you're not used to playing this type of chord.

50. Cool Blues Riff

This riff is similar to the one used in *Jesus Just Left Chicago* by ZZ Top.

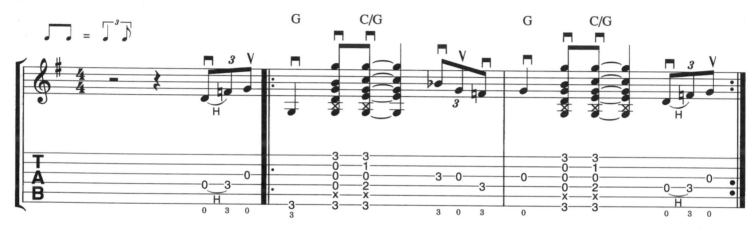

51. Cruisin' Blues Riff

These double-stop chords are used for this riff.

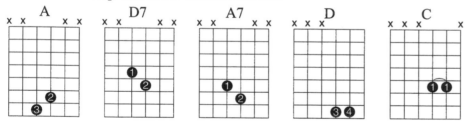

This exciting riff sounds more effective if the double-stop chords are plucked upwards with the middle and ring fingers (middle = *m*, ring = *a*) while the pick strikes the single notes as normal. This pick and fingers combination *(hybrid picking)* is often used by blues and country players. Watch out for the double-stop bend towards the end of the second bar. Here you push the two strings upwards so that the third string is raised by two frets and the second string is raised by one fret.

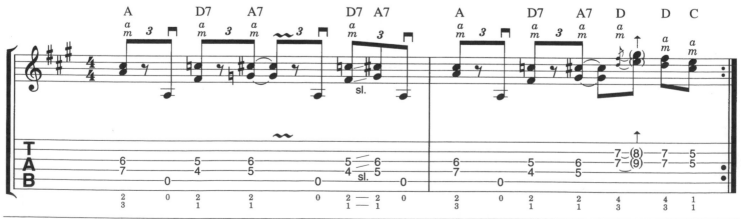

52. Country Blues Riff

The following chords are used in the next riff.

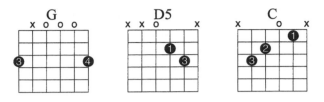

I played this riff on a track called *And My Old Rocking Horse* which appears on the album "Pluto Plus."

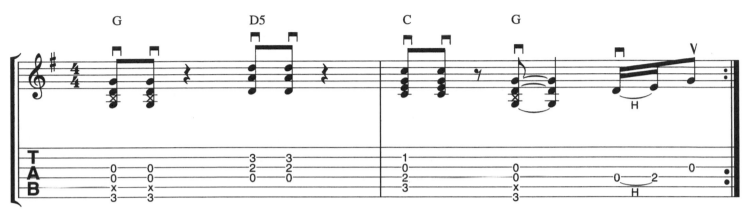

53. Rock Blues Riff

The following chords are used in the next riff.

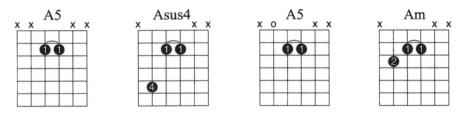

The lower strings are *choked* in the first three bars of the riff shown here. This percussive effect is achieved by hitting the strings with the side of the picking hand (as you pick the strings) while the left-hand fingers are placed across the strings to deaden them.

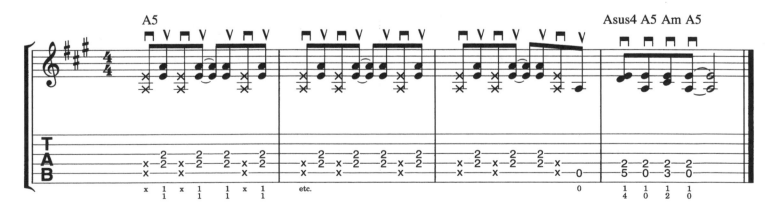

ADVANCED BLUES RUNS

Earlier on we ventured outside the pentatonic box pattern. On this page and the following pages we're going to explore the fretboard even further starting with the following two blues runs.

54. Ascending Blues Run

This run starts on the open E sixth string and progresses all the way up to the twelfth fret of the first string.

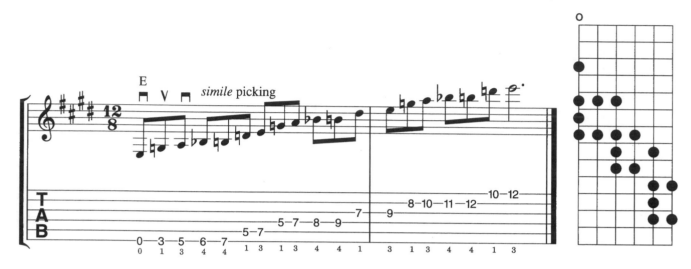

55. Descending Blues Run

Now here's a descending run which starts at the twelfth fret of the first string and finishes on the open sixth string.

56. Descending Blues Run

Here's an exciting run full of chromatic notes which can be used in a fast or slow type of twelve-bar blues.

57. Descending Blues Run

Diminished chords are used to embellish a blues, acting as a link between the main chords. This type of chord substitution is very common in jazz blues and gives an added dimension to the blues sound.

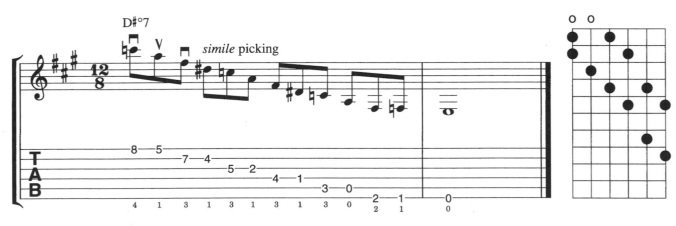

58. Ascending Blues Run

This run uses the notes from the G blues scale.

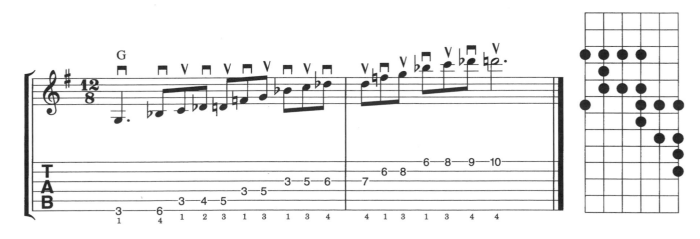

59. Descending Blues Run

The notes for this run come from the G Mixolydian scale (a scale used frequently by modern blues and rock players).

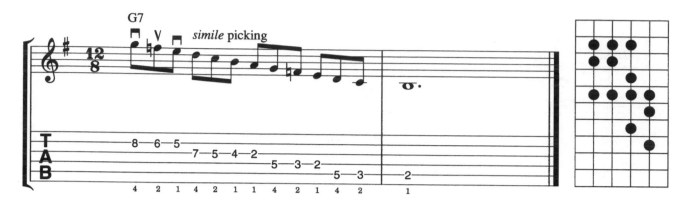

INTROS, OUTROS, AND TURNAROUNDS

60. Intro in G

Double-stops are used throughout this classic blues intro.

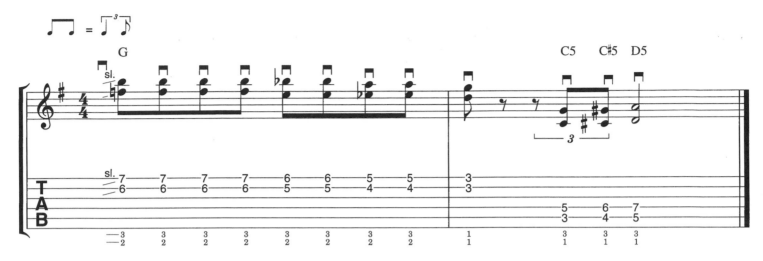

61. Outro in A

A two-fret string bend along with slides, pull-off, hammer-on, and vibrato help to create a great sounding finish to a blues song or solo, but it may take a while to master properly.

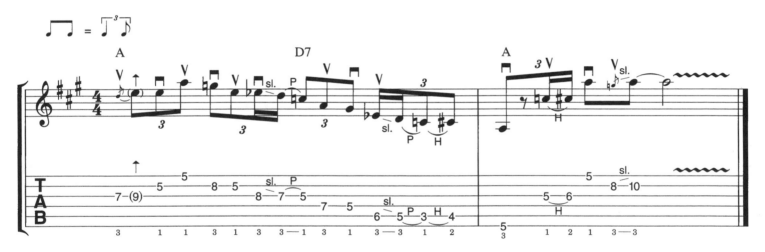

62. Turnaround

Now try this simple but effective turnaround in the key of G.

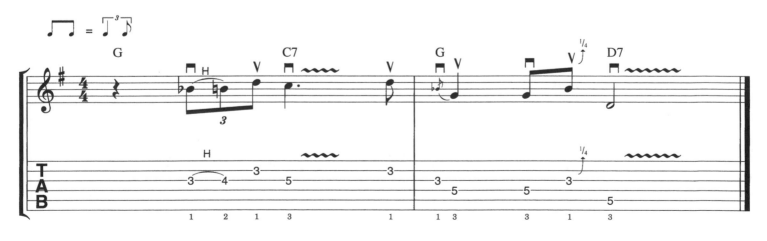

63. Turnaround

This turnaround starts with a two-fret string bend and is very easy to play. (It can be played in B major as well).

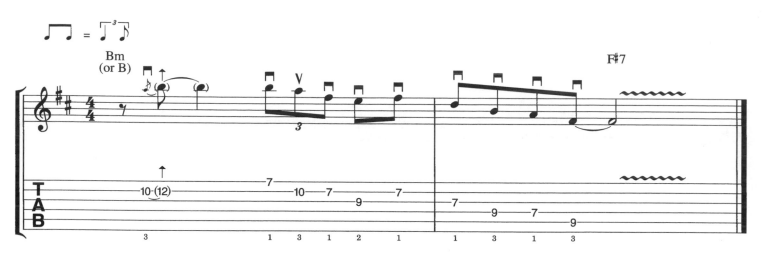

64. Intro in C Minor

Here is an exciting intro in the style of Albert Collins and B.B. King (this will work in C major as well).

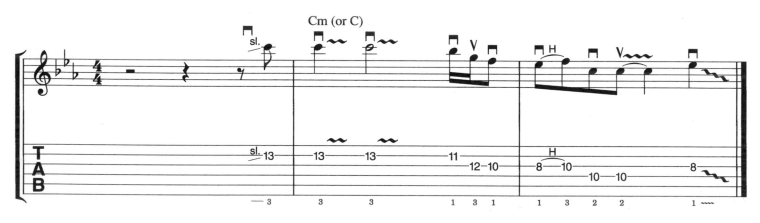

65. Outro in G

The outro shown here is very slow and laid back. The chords in the last measure give it a slightly jazzy sounding finish.

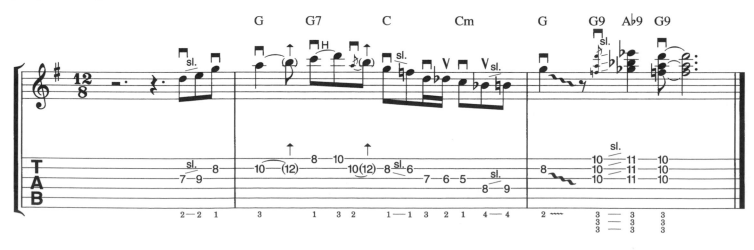

Preparation for *Just Give Me a Call*

Okay! Time to get ready for another solo. The following two riffs act as the main theme throughout the solo.

66. Blues Riff

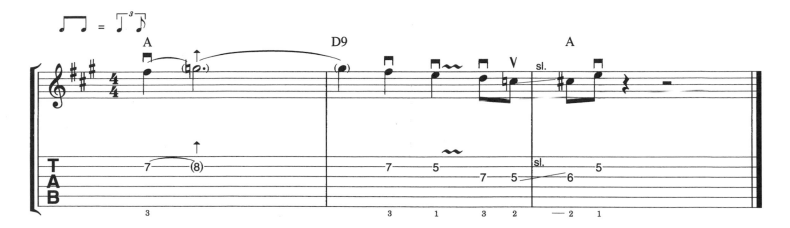

67. Blues Riff

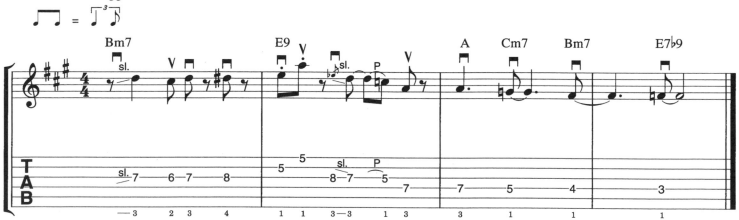

The two licks here are quite long, so remember that you can learn them in sections if you find it easier.

68. Blues Lick

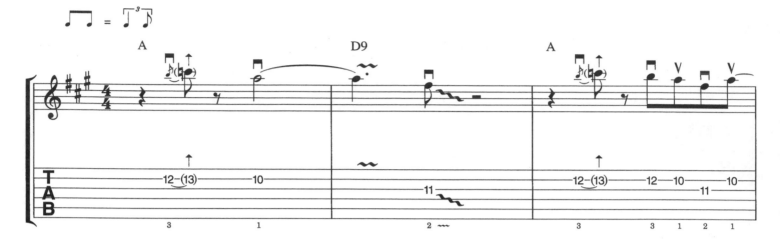

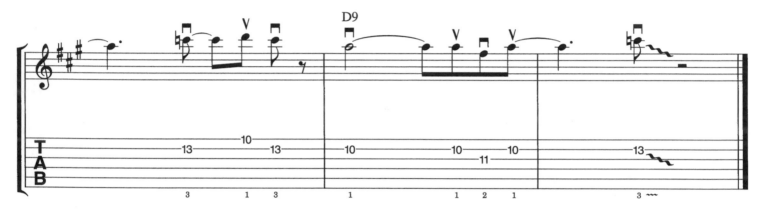

69. Blues Lick

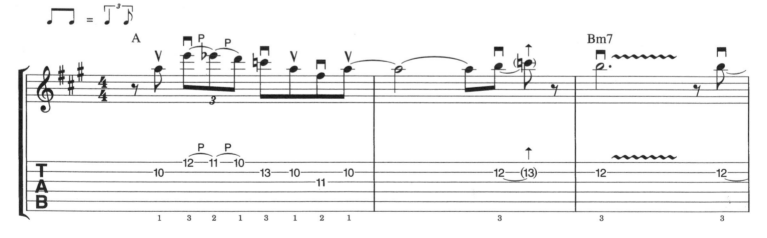

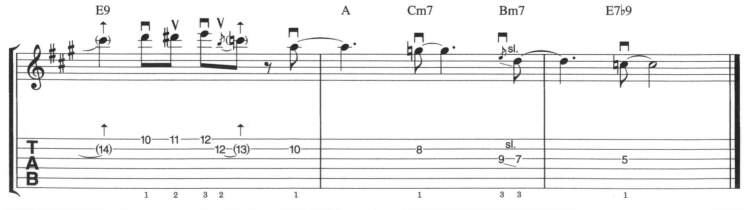

70. Outro Lick

The double-stops and final chord in this outro will sound more effective using your fingers (pick and fingers for the last chord) to pluck the strings but you can use the pick if you prefer.

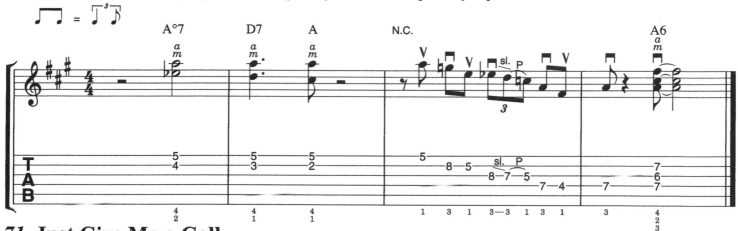

71. Just Give Me a Call

There are four verses to this solo, notice on the last verse (after the two theme riffs) only the first half of blues lick number 67 is played, otherwise its fairly straightforward.

Verse Three

No.68 Blues Lick

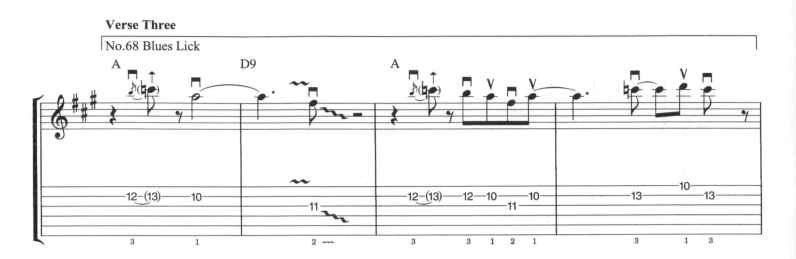

No.68 continued

No.69 Blues Lick

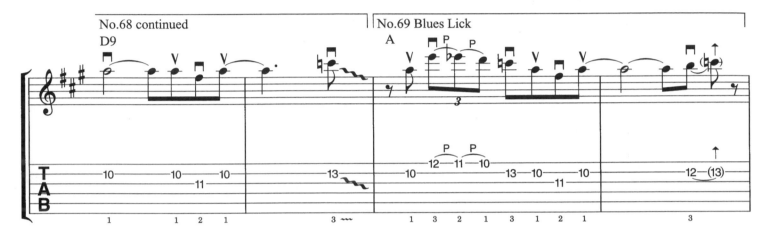

No.69 continued

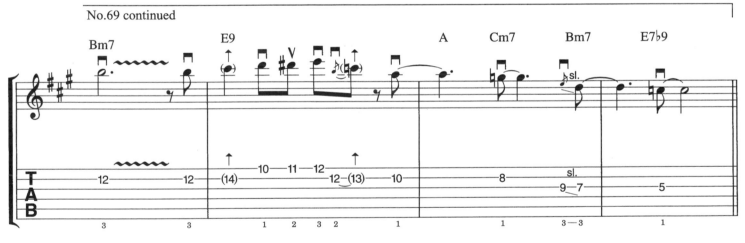

Verse Four

No.66 Blues Riff

72. Five Blues Scale Patterns

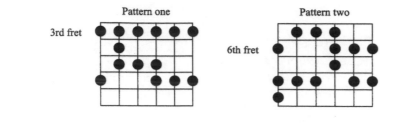

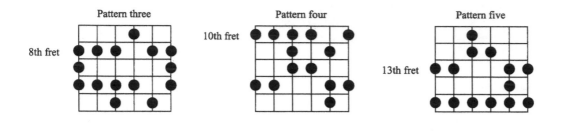

ADVANCED BLUES BENDS

The following blues licks all incorporate advanced string bending techniques such as the three-fret string bend and the pre-bend.

73. Blues Lick

This lick starts with a three-fret upward string bend at the thirteenth fret on the second string using your third finger, as with the string bends earlier on in the book. Remember to reinforce this finger with your second finger.

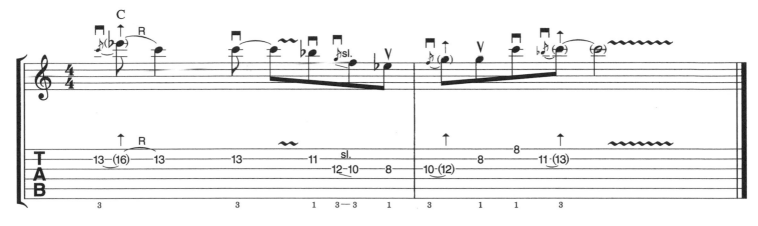

74. Blues Lick

Here's another lick starting with a three-fret bend. This time it's on the first string, so you'll need a bit more strength to push the string up.

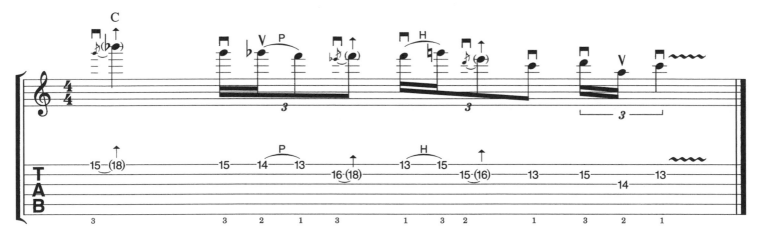

75. Blues Lick

A couple of pre-bends are used here. The first one, as it begins the lick, is quite easy, but the next one, because it follows other notes is more difficult.

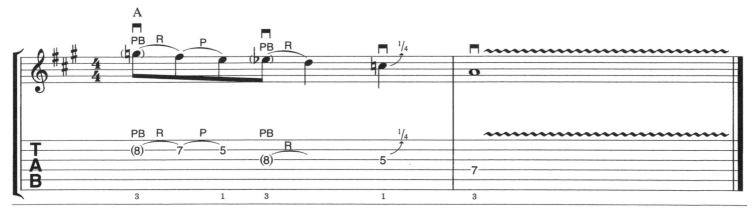

Preparation for *Goin' Back Home*

Here are some licks for the next guitar solo.

76. Blues Lick

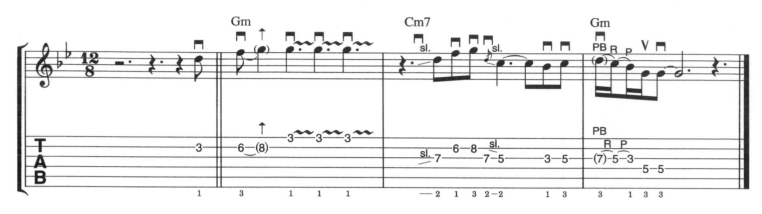

77. Blues Lick and Turnaround

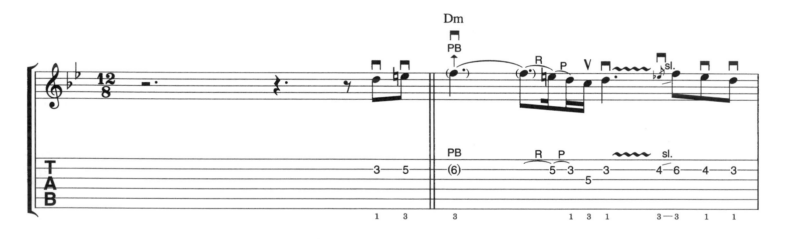

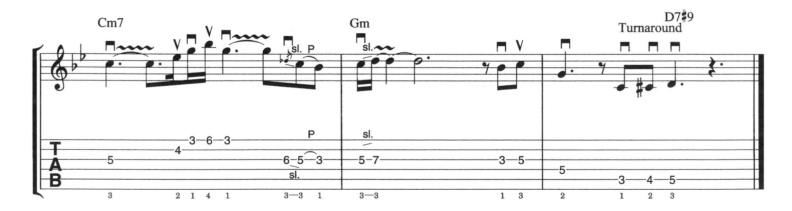

78. Blues Lick

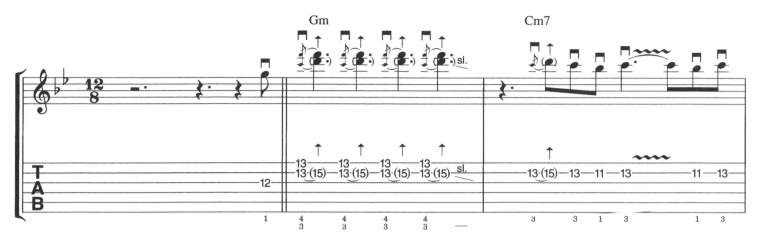

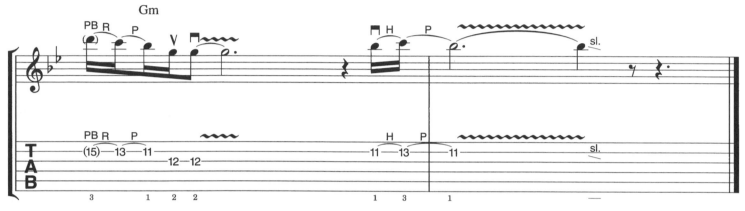

79. Blues Lick

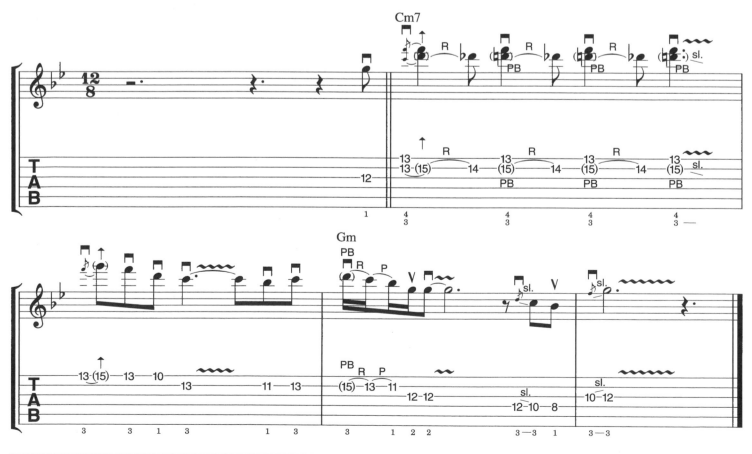

80. Blues Lick and Turnaround

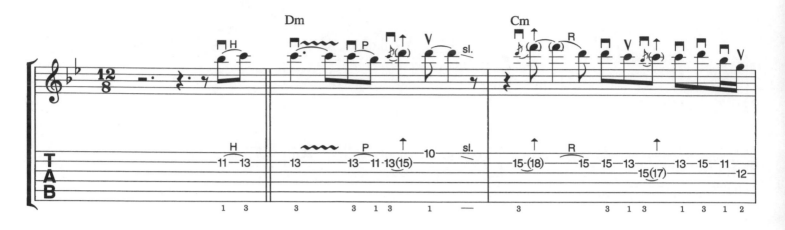

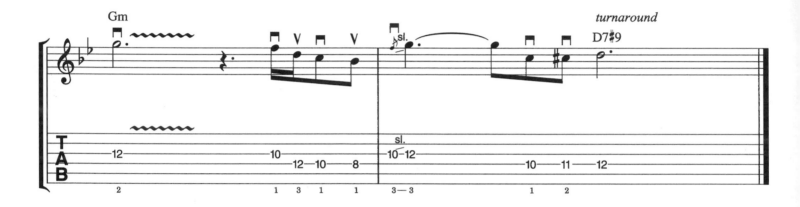

81. Outro Lick

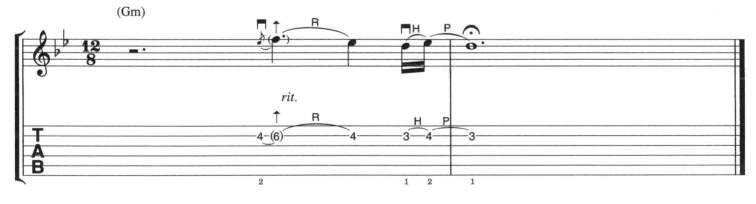

82. Goin' Back Home

Now put the licks from pages 48 through 50 together for this medium paced solo which is in the key of G minor.

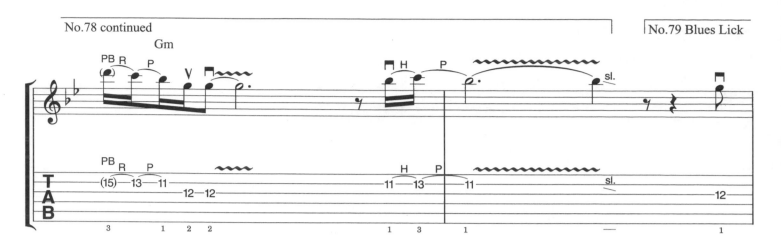

No.79 continued

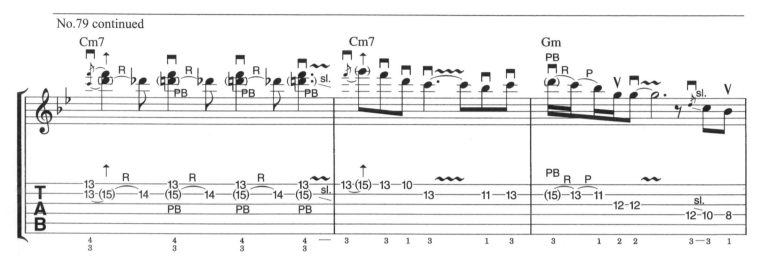

No.79 continued | No.80 Blues Lick & Turnaround

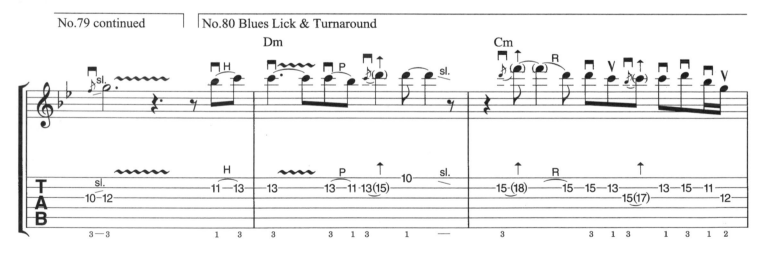

No.80 continued

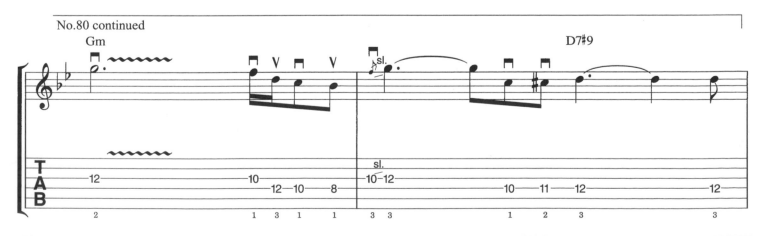

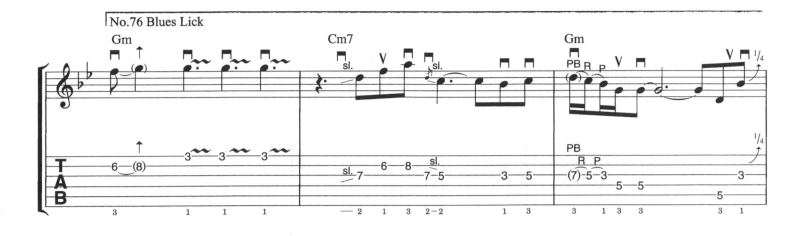

No.76 Blues Lick

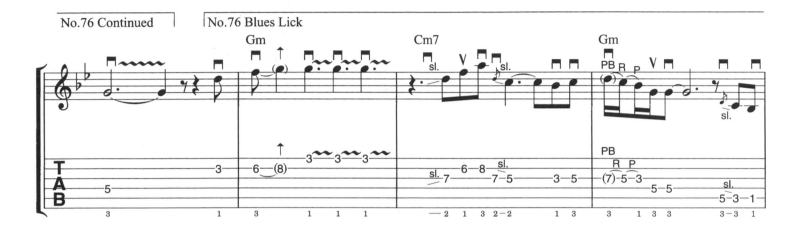

No.76 Continued | No.76 Blues Lick

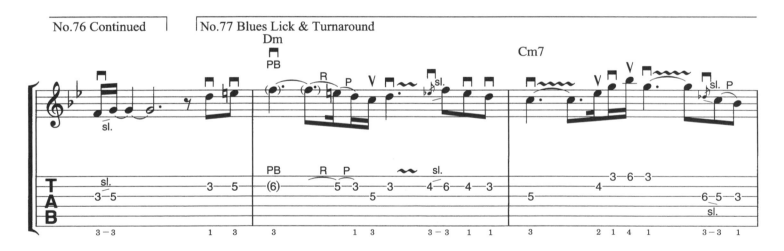

No.76 Continued | No.77 Blues Lick & Turnaround

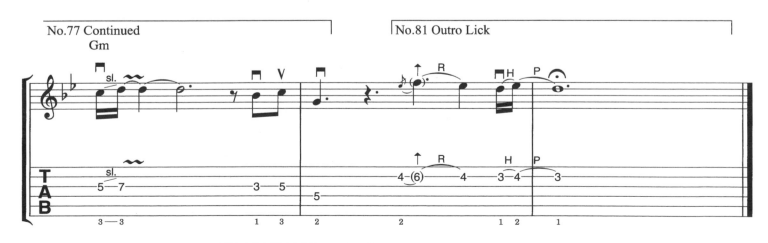

No.77 Continued | No.81 Outro Lick

Constructing a Blues Solo

Now that you've got this far with the book it would be a good time to start making up your own solos. There are no hard and fast rules here. An experienced guitar player can improvise a solo using a selection of tried and trusted blues patterns and licks strung together or by literally making it up as he/she goes along. More often than not, it will be a mixture of both.

Here are some ideas to help you create your own solos.

1. Try listening to a solo by a famous guitarist, such as B.B. King, Eric Clapton, Stevie Ray Vaughan, Peter Green, Buddy Guy, *etc.*, and try to copy the first couple of bars or so. You can then borrow this (to be replaced later on) to set the style and pace for your own solo.

2. Try following this with some blues patterns and licks from this book.

3. Work out some of your own patterns and licks. These can be based on various scales (*i.e.* the pentatonic minor scale, blues scale, *etc.*). Remember however that notes can be sterile and meaningless without some form of rhythm. Also remember the various techniques such as slides, hammer-ons, pull-offs, blues bends, and vibrato can be used to add feel to the notes.

4. Experiment. Don't be afraid to try something out just because it might sound bad—you'll never come up with anything at all if you don't try.

RHYTHM AND PHRASING

Throughout this book you have seen the various riffs, patterns, runs, and licks used to construct each solo.

Here I'd like to show you how you can form your own ideas for creating your own riffs.

The following three examples show each stage in the development of a typical soul-blues riff.

83. Two-bar phrase

The first two bars of the riff are based on this rhythm.

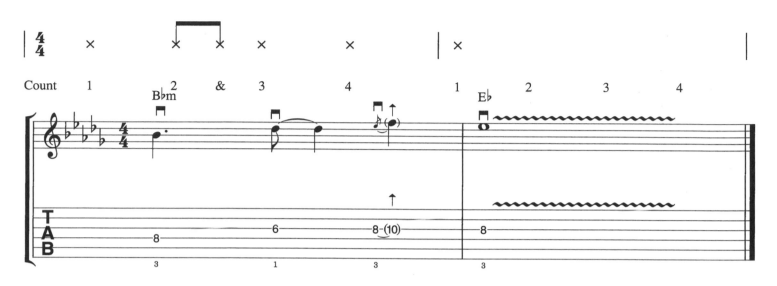

84. Two-bar phrase

This rhythm is used in the next two bars of the riff. Notice the lazy triplets at the start of the first bar. This gives the rhythm a staggered feel.

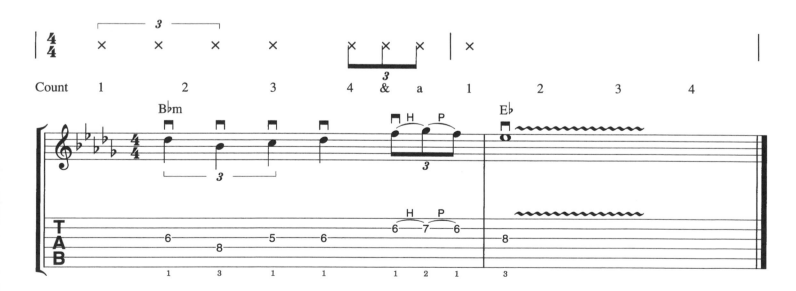

85. Four Bar Phrase

The next four bars are based on this rhythm

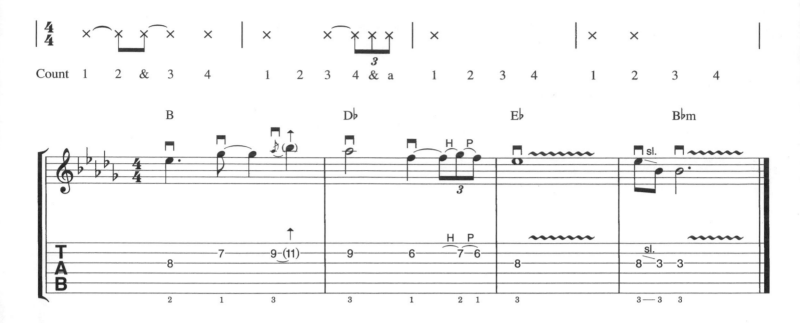

86. Soul Blues Riff

Now put numbers 83, 84, and 85 together to play the entire riff.

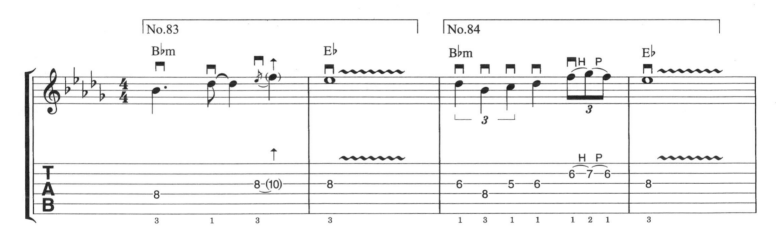

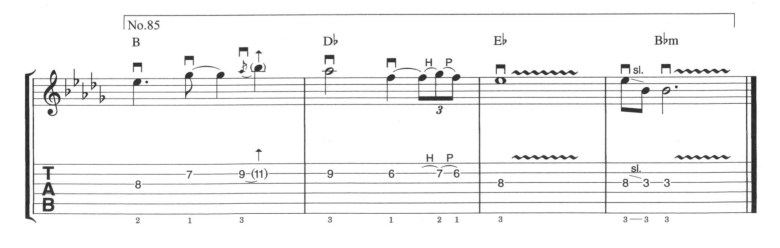

PREPARATION FOR *SO LONG BLUES*

The following licks are used in the next guitar solo *So Long Blues*.

87. Intro Lick

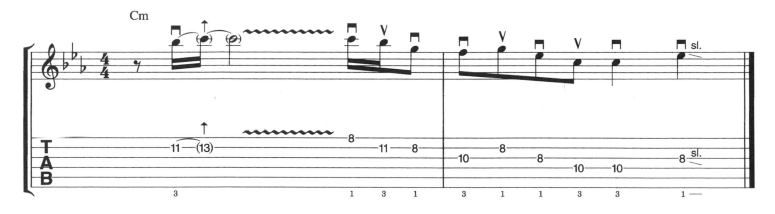

88. Blues Lick

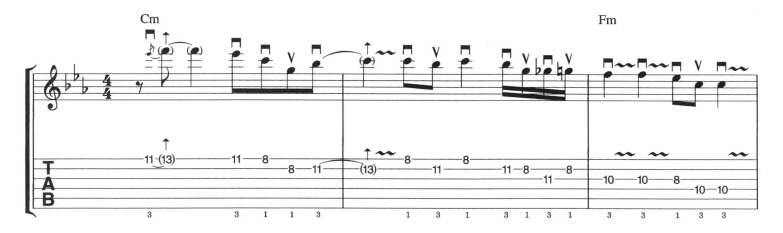

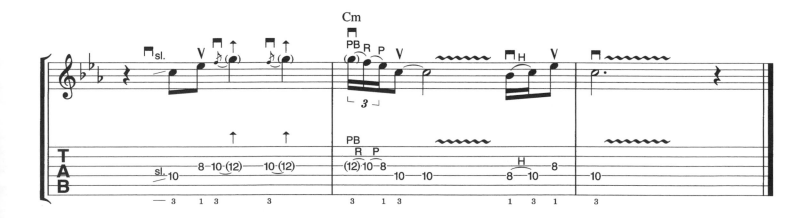

89. Blues Lick & Turnaround

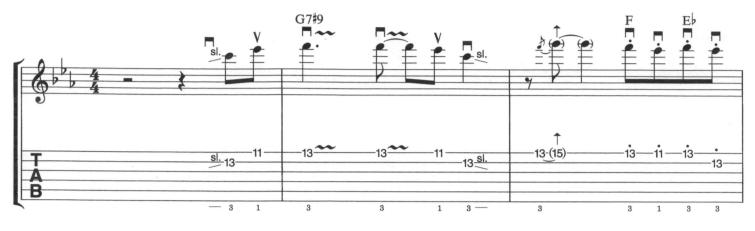

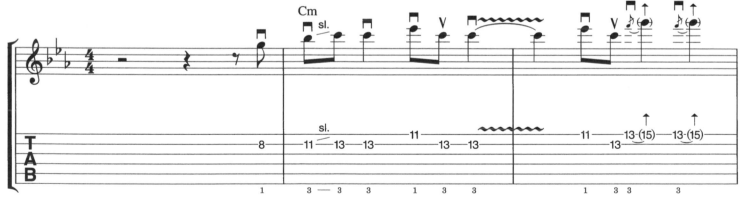

90. Blues Lick

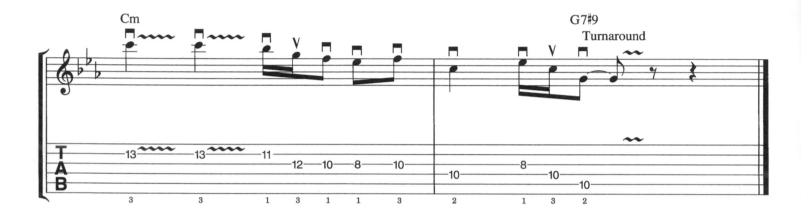

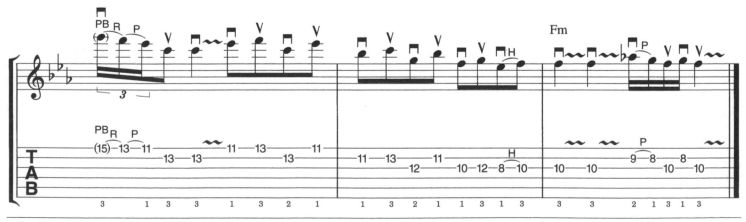

91. Blues Lick & Turnaround

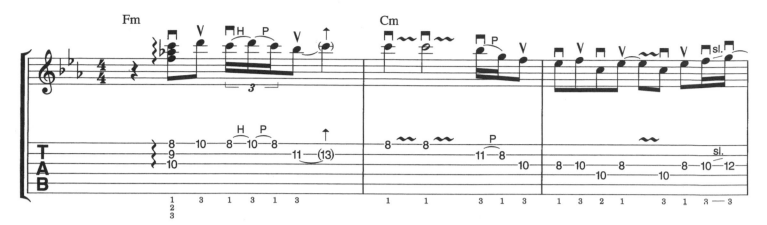

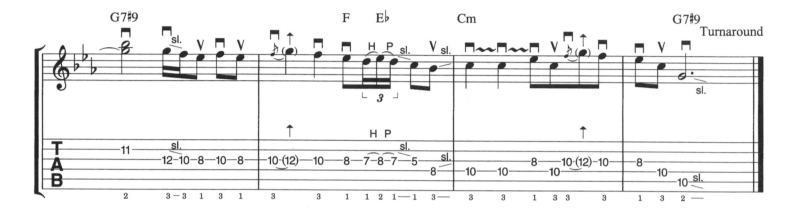

92. Outro Lick

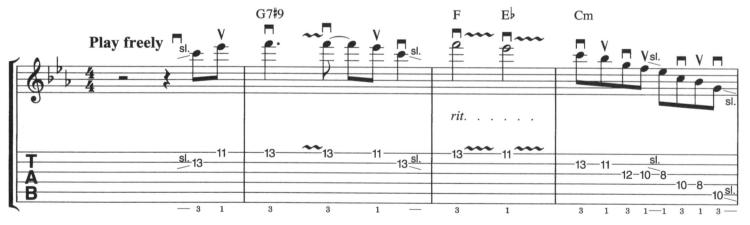

93. So Long Blues

I got the inspiration for this solo by listening to Gary Moore's brilliant version of
Oh Pretty Woman. It's an up tempo blues with plenty of the usual bluesy string bends, hammer-ons,
pull-offs, vibrato, and slide techniques. However, I've kept things a lot simpler than the
abovementioned piece. There are four verses altogether and that tricky outro at the end. Feel free to
try out some of your own ideas here and enjoy yourself.

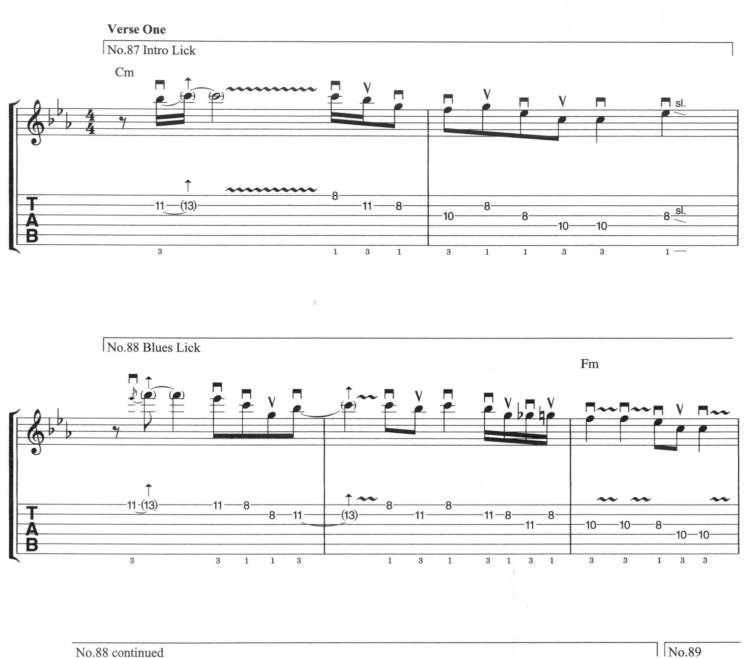

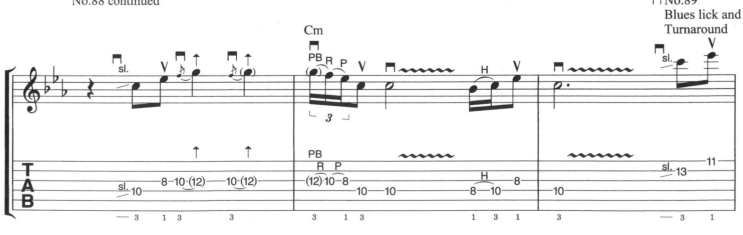

No.89 continued

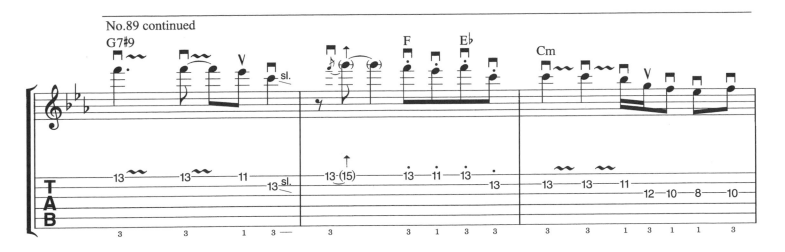

Verse Two

No.89 continued | No.90 Blues Lick

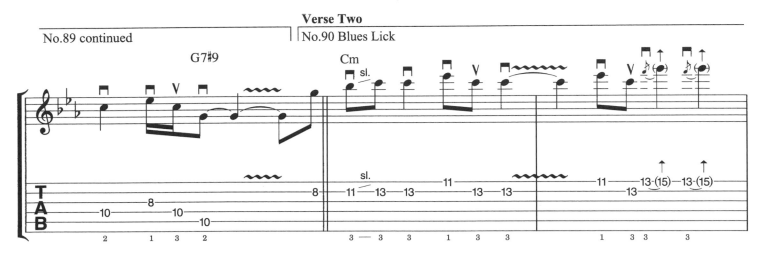

No.90 continued

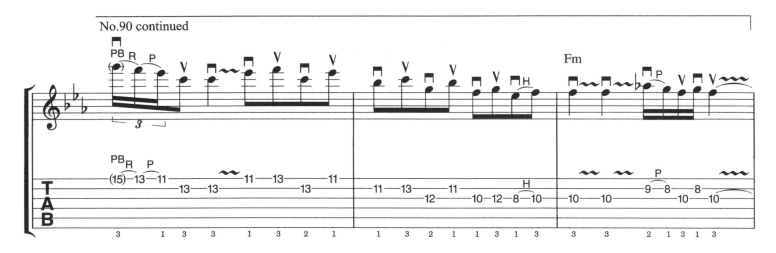

No.91 Blues Lick and Turnaround

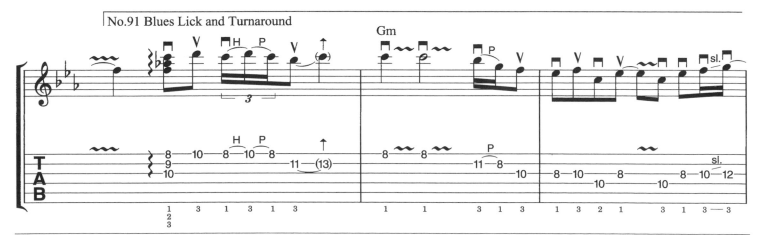

No.91 continued

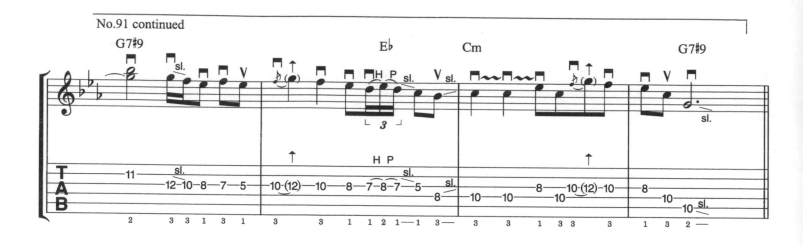

Verse Three

Keyboard Solo

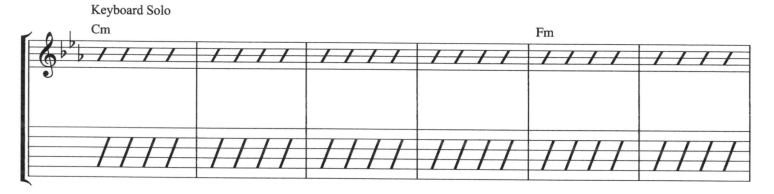

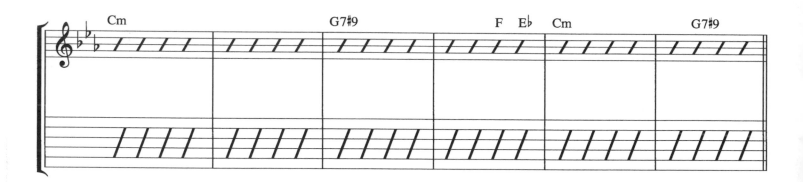

Verse Four

No.87 Intro Lick

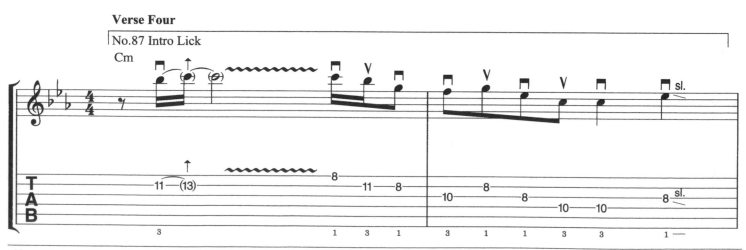

No.88 Blues Lick

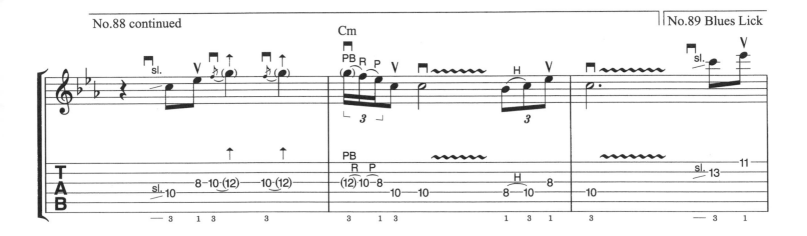

No.88 continued

No.89 Blues Lick

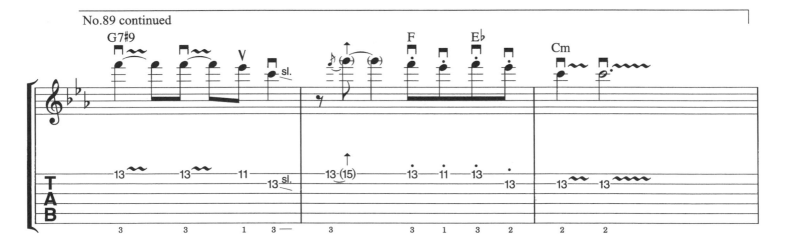

No.89 continued

No.89 Blues Lick & Turnaround

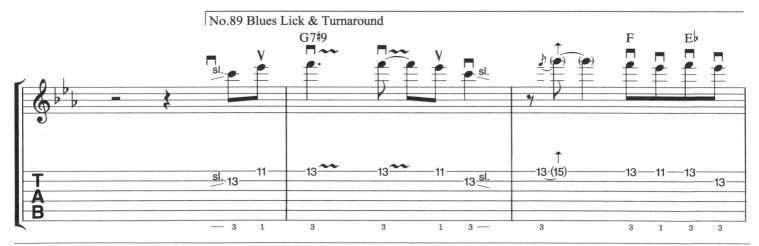

No.89 continued

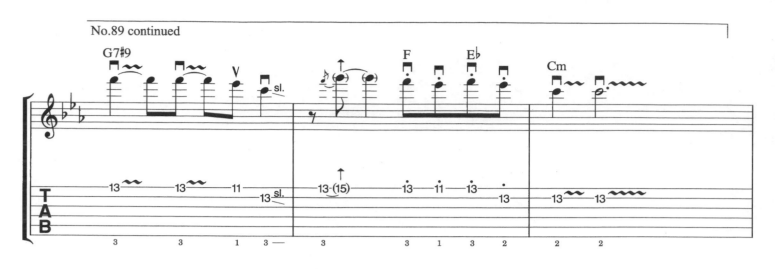

No.92 Outro Lick

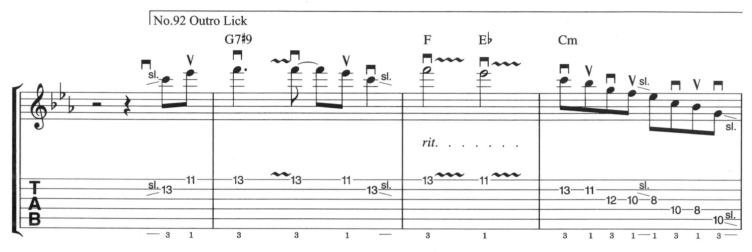

No.92 continued

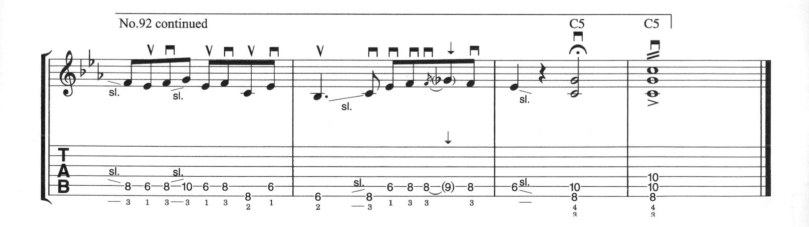